A Glimpse Inside the Shell

Written by: Dr. Zaria L. Cole

A GLIMPSE INSIDE THE SHELL
Copyright © 2021 by DR. ZARIA L. COLE

ISBN: 978-1-7378758-4-0

Library of Congress Control Number: 2021921980

All rights reserved. No part of this publication may be reproduced, distributed, or transmitted in any form or by any means, including photocopying, recording, or other electronic or mechanical methods, without the prior written permission of the publisher or author, except in the case of brief quotations embodied in critical reviews and certain other noncommercial uses permitted by copyright law.

Although every precaution has been taken to verify the accuracy of the information contained herein, the author and publisher assume no responsibility for any errors or omissions. No liability is assumed for damages that may result from the use of information contained within.

Table of Contents

DEDICATION 5
ACKNOWLEDGEMENTS 6
(DARKNESS) THE DAY IS AS DARK AS NIGHT 7
GLIMPSE INSIDE THE SHELL 9
MISUNDERSTOOD 20
WHO AM I? 23
FICKLE 24
WHO'S THE GIRL INSIDE THE SHELL? 5/26/09[BLR1] 27
IN DUE TIME 31
COTTON CANDY 33
FREE TO WRITE 37
FREE TO WRITE PART TWO: I DON'T WANT TO WRITE 39
SEDUCTRESS 42
MEN 45
CAN YOU? 48
CRUSH 49
MIND GAMES 51
ATTRACTION 52
LOVE 53
LYRICAL PENETRATION 54
EROTICA 56
GOODBYE 58
COME AWAY WITH ME 60
IMAGINARY BOYFRIEND 63
PURSUE 65
QUESTIONS 67
UNAVAILABLE 69
I'M READY 71
IT'S DONE 73
THERAPY 77
IT 79
THE LIGHT 81

TRUE LOVE	83
CHEATING	87
PEACE OF MIND	90
THE DOOR	92
HOLY GHOST	94
PERIOD	95
THIS WORLD, THAT WORLD	96
IT'S TIME	98
DEAR GOD	100
FREE TO WRITE PART THREE	104
BUTTERFLY	107
REALLY?	108
DEADLY SIN	110
REUNITED...	114
WEAK	116
PAIN	118
HOPE	119
SIMPLE...	120
LYRICS...	121
EXPERIENCE HIM FOR YOURSELF	122
SCULPTURE PARK	124
PROTECT YOUR MIND	126
REMINDER	128
MY HELP	130
UNCOMFORTABLE	132
FIRE AROUND ME	135
THE SOUND	136
I LOVE YOU, JESUS	139
THE NIGHT IS AS BRIGHT AS THE DAY	142
ABOUT THE AUTHOR	144

Dedication

This book is dedicated to those who feel trapped within themselves. The ones who have so much to say yet feel as though no one is listening.

Acknowledgements

I'd like to thank God for His unyielding love, patience, and tenderness towards me.

My mother Ophelia, for passing her love of writing to me & always supporting my dreams, no matter what they are!

My deceased, yet beloved father Albert Cole Sr., for reading everything I wrote with such interest and love before his passing.

My family, friends, and supporters!

(DARKNESS) The Day is as Dark as Night

Insecure. Shy. Passive.
My tears are the only sounds.
Surrounding me.
There is no joy.
There is no hope.
I am a beautiful masterpiece gone unnoticed
Even with eyes shut tight,
The day is as dark as night.
That is my life.
Scared. Intimidated. Confused.
I am walking. Talking. Breathing.
Yet there is no life in me.
I cry. No one dries my eyes.
I shout. No one responds…
I surround myself with people.
Only to be left alone.
Even with eyes wide shut,
The day is as dark as night.
This is my life.
Numb. Weak. Desperate.
Accept Me.
Embrace me.
SEE me.
I am here.
Please,

Just Love me.
My flag is raised.
Jesus.
Sweet, sweet Jesus.
Help me, please.

Glimpse Inside the Shell

Take a glimpse inside the shell of this withdrawn girl.
Do you think you can handle my world?
Let's go back to the beginning,
I was so outgoing and carefree.
Completely oblivious to what the world had in store for me.
I was giddy with joy, until the enemy of my soul sold me a lie & I began to unfold

You see skirts and dresses were the things I was most impressed with…
Lip stick & frolicking around
Laughter & giggles were my known sounds

The enemy painted a picture that those around me,
were so resilient, so carefree
I was deemed sensitive, they were deemed tough
They said I cared too much, I felt they didn't care enough
I was delicate,
I didn't like to get dirty and was often sick.

I began to believe the lie that I was alone,

That others didn't care.
I felt people were happiest when I wasn't there.
I began to cling to men, especially my brothers,
even the youngest who I once tried to smother.
Throughout the years I tried to win acceptance
But I just ate away my pain with great diligence.
The bigger my waist expanded
The more love I secretly demanded

But I was so good at hiding that other's couldn't see. People didn't know the pain growing inside me.
My bff, I hid it from her the most, in fact all she saw was me pulling away from her even though we remained close.
She thought I just had an attitude, mean & reclusive whose heart she couldn't capture
But I wasn't those things, I was a girl lost in her own rapture.

As a teen my desire for love and acceptance had become almost obsessive.
But I hid it so deeply, to find it you'd need a

detective.
To really see the pain behind the smile.
The pain of a misguided child.

Bitterness surrounding me, I just wanted
someone to set me free.
Anyone to love me beyond my outer shell.
Anyone these dark secrets I could trust
enough to tell.

But was the pain I felt real?
Abandoned by love?
Was I really hated for the way I looked?
Did those closest really view me as stranger
in their heart as if I were a crook?
Does it really matter if they did or didn't?
The fact that I believed it has now made me
resistant
to the concept of a healthy relationship.
Which is why I believe it's so easy for people
to abandon ship
to leave me unguarded, take away their love
but really sometimes I pushed away, I
shoved.
I did not want their tainted love.

So I became a fortress, keeping all forms of it

away.
I was not a team player, it had to be my way.
But there was something I could give freely,
and that was the most precious parts of me,
my body.
I gave it away in pieces and sections
and the powerful feeling I got from it was like
my own little slice of heaven.
The men chased me, they wanted more.
Sadly, I'd become an attention whore
It wasn't sex, just me leaving them thinking.
But I was the one in actuality sinking
lower, and lower into a deep dark depression,
opening the door wider and wider for my own
oppression.
I was a woman scorned.
Scorned from people and the way my heart
burned.
I was so wrong, but yet I felt so right.
I felt it was okay to sneak away into the night.
To get the acceptance and attention I desired
I mistakenly felt loved, but I was no better
than a whore for hire.
Date after Date,
I took advantage of nice guys who didn't
want to keep me out late,
and I thought I was getting over because they

always paid
even though… they never got laid.
I may not have screwed anyone else,
into a lack of intimacy,
into a series of heart injuries.
An empty canvas I build myself up with wasted vanities.
Relationships going nowhere.
Surrounding myself with people I knew didn't care.
I was too afraid to do what was right.
To stay up working on things that actually mattered through the night.
Instead I stayed up web flirting in chat rooms.
Opening the door for hidden lust for my soul to consume.
I gave up my chance for true knowledge,
for I was too afraid to go away to college.
I lacked real confidence.
True self-worth wasn't in my present tense.
I didn't know who I was or who I wanted to be.
And the feelings I got from men was enough for me.
But soon I got tired of the things that didn't last.
I noticed I was in a cycle, ghost of relationships past.

To make matters worse I'd become sick.
To my surprise it was the benefit of being "thick".
No one believed the pain at first.
Some believed it was just another way to feed my attention thirst.
But no, it wasn't something I did for humor.
I was diagnosed with a brain tumor.
But it wasn't the kind that actually grew.
Just something for my self-esteem to further undo.
I didn't care if I lived or died.
But I was pleasantly surprised to see people around me cry.
Not because I wanted them to be in pain,
but because it gave me a little sense of worth again.
To me it was proof that people actually cared.
Unfortunately it wasn't enough to keep me here.
Often, I delayed exercise or medicine,
there was even a time I mixed my pills with gin.
But it just made me sleepy instead of feeling high.
And then I discovered I could actually die.
It should have scared me, but it made me feel free.

This was my chance to make my own history.
But I just couldn't do it,
not for lack of trying, I just always blew it,
so, instead I took my desire to God.
Lord please free me from this happy façade.
Each morning I was disappointed that my prayer wasn't answered,
having life meant more and more banter.
Then something happened that I couldn't comprehend.
My relationship with my father came to a dramatic end.
He lost his battle with life.
It's hard for me to say the words, but my father is no longer alive.

And that left me feeling even more unwanted.
Because the one person I didn't have to make love me had checked out for his last appointment.
If I thought I was sad before,
I needed to brace myself for what was now in store.
Although they were backstabbers, I kept these people around
But with my daddy gone, I had no need to keep these friendships sound.
One by one I picked them off my list.

I'd rather be alone then surrounded by fake bliss.

In this time I found comfort in a guy,
but I had no idea he was the master of all lies.
He seemed so innocent and into me.
But he was a master magician, I was deceived.
It took me years to get over what I let happen,
and my hopes of finding real love where completely done with then.
I didn't trust anyone, not men not women.
There was no one new that my heart could be given.
I was lost.
Hurt,
and felt alone.
Time passed by and I barely left home.
I was totally misguided, blinded by my pain,
I replayed life's trials over and over again.
My life had become stagnated.
Caught in a gang where heartbreak was ignited.
I was distraught by this mess.
Mad at a foe I didn't know was myself.
And now, now I see,
that the changes my life needed have always been inside me.

Now I know to take time to reflect,
to heal and mend and allow the Lord to protest.
The thoughts that once plagued me and kept me bound,
to sexual prowess and the hidden sounds,
that can only be heard in the spirit realm,
the things that secretly attract them.
There are people who prey on wounded souls.
Wolves in sheep's clothing, who desire to keep you in their hold.
Now I know to take the time to build my confidence.
To work hard on retraining my thoughts with fierce diligence.
Now I know that the love and acceptance I desire, that I need, that the changes my life needed have always be inside me.
Now I know to take time to reflect.
To heal and mend and allow the Lord to protest.
The thoughts that once plagued me and kept me bound
to sexual prowess and the hidden sounds,
that can only be heard in the spirit realm,
the things that secretly attract them.
There are people who prey on wounded souls.
Wolves in sheep's clothing, who desire to

keep you in their hold.
Now I know to take the time to build my confidence.
To work hard on retraining my thoughts with fierce diligence.
Now I know that the love and acceptance I desire, that I need
lies in the arms of the father, just waiting for me to plant the seeds.
Seeds of righteousness, seeds of truth.
Seeds of Holy, open rebuke.
For the traps and plans the enemy has for me, the serpents open desire to keep me from being free.
Now I know to build up my self-love and worth
to keep on the path of ultimate self-growth,
now I know to take the path of true joy
that I don't get intimacy from being some man's little toy.
This path to redemption is not simple,
and I'm learning there's more to me than my charm and cute dimples.
I am something special, someone who I myself am learning to embrace,
and I know that I'm not left alone to endure this race.

It will take steadfast thoughts
and an open heart for God to join me on this walk.
I have forgiven my bestie for our differences
and am coming to accept my bigger appearance.
I have let go of all the men and friends who
played my heart like an old piano,
and it's not so bad to explore my gifts solo.
God has given me a time to myself
to get myself together, to be my best.
I am much stronger today than my yesterday.
And I am learning to train my irrational
mindset to behave in God's way.
I am working on the things that I allowed to become me.
I am working on being the me I was always supposed to be.
I am a work in progress.
Moving from a girl to a woman controlling her stress.
I digress.
I am me,
I am Lacy,
and thankful for a real chance to be free.

Misunderstood

What time is it? Nearly midnight, time for
most to call it a night,
but not me, not Lacy.
I'm on a mission to be free.
Though I barely got any sleep,
I must stay up until I am complete.
I hate being the way I was.
Tired of being bullied by love.
A lack of passion was once my crime.

Now here I am jotting down rhyme after
rhyme.

I'm tired of being misunderstood and taken
for granted.
I'm tired of my own view on love and life,
which is often slanted.
I wish for a brighter, better tomorrow.
So here I am writing out my sorrow.

It's not so hard to see why people are
confused by me,
with no idea of who I am or who I aim to be.
It's kind of depressing but I must keep
pressing.
Yes, I have to keep going.

Because this time I am going to show them.
But not just them, I have to also show myself.
That I have what it takes to pass this test,
I am tired of this particular cycle,
I am unique, the opposite of typical.

And I want something more, so I'm doing something different.
And I know it will pay off because I'm being very diligent.
Every time I'm reminded of the past,
I change my course of action because the old ones didn't last.

Being misunderstood has it perks and rewards.
I'm learning that I don't have to fight; I can put down my sword.
No need to be so defensive.
My wounds are already deep and extensive.

No need to add insult to injury,
I'm learning how to let God go to war for me.

I can only do so much.
Like being cleansed of my demons, including lust.

Yes, I can admit my faults.
Admitting when you're wrong helps strengthen your walk.
So, as I sit sometimes all alone.
Misunderstood, but on my own throne.
I have to remember who is always there.
Who'll never leave, who'll always care.
My friend who sticks closer than a brother.
Jesus, whose love keeps me sober.

Who Am I?

Intuitive, Caring, Sharing,
but very rarely daring.
Loving, Loyal, Kind,
but often run the risk of being blind
to the realities of life.
That sometimes people really do intend to cause strife.
That sometimes the best thing is to walk away.
Because nine times outta ten we won't have the right thing to say.
Until hours, sometimes days after
but by then we'll be on to our next disaster.
A shelled woman could be the best thing to come into your life.
Once she's tamed her emotions, she'll make the best wife.
Just be sure not to be the main cause of her grief.
Or she'll steal your soul like a common thief.
Yes, she may be vengeful and full of pride,
but if you can avoid her bad side, you'll enjoy her ride,
because she'll be the best lover you've ever and will ever have.

Fickle

You know that old saying people come and go?
Well, I don't think they meant it for what I'm going through.
You see, I get close to someone, I let them in.
They withdraw, and I hide my feelings, zen.
But it does bother me, I do wonder why someone once close, becomes a stranger in the night.
Sometimes I get the courage to ask if I've offended them,
maybe, perhaps I murdered their character?
But it's always the same story, just a different chapter,
"Oh no, you haven't done anything wrong…"
In my mind I'm thinking so you're just a cold-hearted drone?
Incapable of intimacy?
I thought I was beyond this cycle, silly me…
It's funny because people leave, but always come back,
and look at me funny when I say I'm done with that…
Done with being your emotions rag doll.
One minute you love me, the next you stall me out. As if my feelings don't exist.

Take you back? NO WAY! I don't have time for this,
I'm so tired of fickle friendships, where I'm up on a pedestal.
If I look at you funny, I'm now worse than the devil.
People don't give me any headway, no rope, no room for error.
I'm supposed to be the nice girl, the bigger person forever.
I'm shattered...
I can't live up to the pressure.
I'm literally drowning in other people's tears, and carrying the scars of such abuse over the years.
I'm a person, just like you,
except now when I have a problem with someone, I try to stay true
to the creed I've created for myself.
I'm going to tell you about you and your mess instead of just distancing myself and walking away.
You may not like it, but I'm going to say what I need to say.
And after everything is all said and done
if you don't like my words, you can then be gone.

But to just drop off, to lose contact without a reason, no notice,
is the ultimate offense to me, but many people don't know this.
Anyway, you who have gone cold, go ahead, stay in your icy zone.
And when you come back, trying to get back in my good grace
I'm sincerely going to tell you that I still love you, but send you on your way.
Your actions prove that you think my friendship is overrated
So I'll do us both a favor and love you from the distance you created.

Who's the Girl Inside the Shell?
5/26/09

She sits there anticipating the sting of heartbreak,
strangled by fear with each step she tries to take.
Her heart beats and beats and beats for a love she can't seem to reach.
Insecurities rule her world,
her thoughts all mixed up like an ice cream swirl.
She yearns for someone to appease the pain inside,
but, by her rules they must abide.
She feels alone, an outcast in her own soul.
There is no reward for how hard she toils and breaks her back to help others.
She is a prized possession waiting for her discovery.
She can't breathe for trying to stand against the agony of not fitting in.
Instead, she retreats to her shell within.

She desires to overcome the strongholds
but, under the pressure of her own emotions she folds.
Reserved by Nature,

she wonders how others can register
her sweetness, but not her desire for acceptance?
With her loyalty, but seem to take for granted
her other star qualities.
She supports her friends, and protects her family.
But, to cross this shelled girl is a major tragedy
for she finds it hard to forgive, hard to let go.
Therefore, to disrespect her emotional fortress
will leave your life in sorrow.
She eternalizes what has happened, what's been said.
And once she's offended, the offender may
feel as if he's left her for dead.
She won't be able to discern
why you've done her wrong.
Why she attaches so quickly
will remain a mystery.
And she can't comprehend why a friendship
would dissipate.
So all the love she once felt, though real, will
quickly turn to hate.
She'll turn on you worse than an enemy,
and you'd never see it coming from someone
who seemed so sweet.
She hates change, fears it, loathes the idea.

Everything should remain constant, clear, sheer.
She needs to feel secure by her surroundings, her peers.
She needs commitment to feel free to endear.
She needs attention, love, and support.
Although not found of it, manipulation she will resort
to get what she wants, what she feels she deserves,
She isn't afraid to store up her reserves.
Her kind, caring free spirit,
she only gives freely to those she feels are of good merit.
All others are only allowed a preview
of how great she can make the world and all she can do.
She is very cautious of who she lets in
so, she often plays with the heart like a scorned magician.
Giving the tarnished illusion that she cares.
Presumptuously proclaiming that she wants to be there.
When in fact she is waiting to see if it's safe for her to share,
because another rejection, she simply can't bear.

But this butchered butterfly can never truly be free
until she embraces the awesome wonder that is she.
And it is only then that she can show this world
the unflinching beauty of being a reclusive girl.

In Due Time

There's so much on my mind today, as I sit at my desk and let my mind play, it wanders into the abyss of what could be, of who I am, and the things the Lord is allowing me to see.
There's so much that I want, so much I desire, so much I've lost, so many people gone, it stings like fire or an old love song.
So Lord, I ask, what is it that I'm doing wrong?
Things come into my grip, just to be taken away, and what makes it so bad is it's the same thing happening just on a different day.

Cycles. I'm tired of cycles; have I not been a good disciple, of my heart? Of my body? Of my time... sometimes, I wish I could just press rewind.
Then I would never come to a place of surrender, where I could instead rest in the Lord's love that's ever so tender.
I know in due time these things I desire will come to be.
They will materialize into the beautiful images of fulfilled prophecy.
Because God promised me, and for me not to trust Him would be such a tragedy.

What he has for me, it is for me and nothing, not you, he, or she can take from me what is destined to be.
So, as I hold my heart in my own hands, I release it to the only one who can mend the places that are broken and restore a spirit that was once my prized token.
As the Lord does His work in me and takes me through things, I'm not quite ready to see, I will be strong, I will be bold, I will allow His process to flow and take hold.
I will not cry for the things that have passed, broken friendships and relationships that didn't last. I will trust the Lord for and through all things, for if He brought me this far His power can restore... *if* those things are truly meant to be, and if not, I still won't fret because I know that in due time, the things that are supposed to be, will be.

Cotton Candy

I remember in middle school when I first met you; you were sitting at your desk looking a little aloof. Although it was only the first day of school, I still knew that you and I would be cool.

As we became friends, I was happy to know someone else so silly
you laughed at everything,
from all my jokes from my crazy dances to my little toy mouse, Billy.
We quickly became inseparable, and it sounds kind of funny, but our connection was remarkable.

We were both the chubby chicks, but we were nice to everyone, and we didn't mesh with cliques.

In high school the saga continued, we happily carried our friendship on to a new venue.
But sadly things wouldn't stay this blissful for long, because along came a guy who changed our song.
In the beginning, I supported, but it wasn't long before the accusations started.

There were rumors of jealousy and I couldn't understand how you'd think that of me.
If I could ever get you to see that I simply felt you were no longer who I knew you to be.
It became two worlds, you with him, vs. you with your girls.

I tried to let it go, but everything I was feeling kept growing, and growing and so,
I distanced myself from the person you'd become. And I'm sure it seemed silly to some,
But they weren't there for the start of our production, sad to say, but it was beyond construction.

I'm sorry; I suffered from something called 'holding it all in'. I should have been open with you from the beginning. I should have just told you how I felt at the time. Instead of spending my nights wanting to press rewind.

But I digress, I was definitely a work still in progress.
When you went away to school, I really hoped we'd come back cool. But even though you'd apologized, I still couldn't figure out

why I held on so dearly to the destruction that
was all so silly.
I'd already eternalized everything that was
said, everything that was done.
I remember being left out of your graduation,
your senior dedication page.
His friends being mentioned instead of me is
the thing that had my mind so plagued.
We tried to keep it going, but things had
changed,
I felt friendship was far out of our range.
I'm sorry dear cotton candy,
I questioned your ability
and if indeed you were a friend to me?
In my heart, you were my best friend,
and the spot you filled I never allowed
anyone else in.

But dear cotton candy, it's time for my heart
to mend.
It's time to start fresh and let go of what
happened then.

I know that you're happy now,
and I'm on that path too,
but I believe it'll start once I let go of you.

And the countless others who I believe broke my trust.
Bury it in the ground, let it collect its dust.
A lot of what we went through was my own denial
and I'm sorry to miss the birth of your first child.
But everything happens for a reason,
I guess it just came to the end of our season.
And with all the good and sad in the world,
I am happy to have known you,
Ms. Cotton Candy Girl.

Free to Write

What am I feeling today? What is my mind attempting to display?
Why do I carry around this Burden? As if there is no freedom in serving.
If I take my mind off what I feel I miss, then I can escape this eternal abyss.
Where there is nothing, nothing, nothing but pain.
Nothing, nothing, nothing but rain.
But I can be free, freedom is right here waiting for me.
If I close my eyes and let the feelings wander, roam, float, glide into the beautiful skies.
The fears that burn within will no longer reside.

Jesus, Jesus, Jesus, Jesus,
I call your name like a chant at the Cards baseball game.

Jesus, Jesus, Jesus, Jesus,
I need you today, tomorrow, and every day to save us,
save them, save me.
As long as I have Jesus then I can, will, I am free.

So, what am I thinking of today? What is my mind attempting to say?
My heart is beating, wanting to declare,
that the timid feeble girl no longer lives here!

Free, free, free, free.
Free to live, free to breathe.
Free, free, free, free
Free from insecurity, free from the fear to be.
My heart still desires to be liberated.
That my mind has been rejuvenated.

So, what is on *your* heart today? What is *your* mind attempting to display?

Free to Write Part Two: I Don't Want to Write

I don't feel up to this fight.
I wish to just sleep,
sleep away this misery.
Tonight, was mystical.
I tried a new approach; I was rational.
I did make one mistake,
I texted my ex hoping to escape.
This feeling that he doesn't care,
hoping his feelings of remorse and hurt are still there.
But to my expectation, I was right.
He responded with simplicity and that was that for the rest of the night.
Not one phone call? Not one text message?
I know I should look at it as a blessing,
but I'm struggling to get past the anger.
And I know I need to regroup,
I'll stay in resentment while he's out wearing suits.
I'll stay in bondage thinking it's unfair,
while he's out stroking his new wife's hair.
I'll remain single and unable to mingle,

for always thinking how he just shut off his feelings.
While he's out there experiencing new tingles.
So, no, I have to be careful
and allow this to end itself without being regretful.
This is all God's plan
and there's nothing to be mad at, cause my ex wasn't fully a man.
He was, however, the best I've had
but not the best to come.
So, I'm closing my eyes with peace, and being thankful that it's done.

THE OPPOSITE OF SEX: POEMS ABOUT MEN

Seductress

Her eyes lured him in
and the subtle seduction begins.
He never saw it coming,
never imagined a woman could have him running
from store to store to find evidence of how much he adores
her very presence.
He never imagined from a simple woman
he'd need deliverance.
She very playfully touched his collar
knowing full well she's the center of his desire.
She pouts so seductively
playing her game so effortlessly.

He can't resist even the thought of her kiss,
her lips so soft, so moist.
He knows when he feels them he'll simply rejoice.
How long must he wait? How much enticing
can one man take?

She knows that he's getting weak.
She ponders with the idea of giving just a sneak peek

of the simplest form of her that's ever so sweet.
She motions for him to come closer
knowing that with one touch, he'll never desert her.

He moves his mouth inches from her lips
but quickly looks down, he can't believe this.
He backs away quickly with a hint of embarrassment
There it was, and with a quiet explosion, there it went.
She smiles coyly reassuring him, "Baby, it's okay."
We were moving a little fast to play anyway…
She stands to wrap her arms around the shoulders of her man
and begins her seduction over again.

He can't believe he's feeling so good.
He thought what just happened would have ruined the mood.
But looking into her eyes made him feel a certain kind of way
that perhaps this was love, yes this was the way
a man is supposed to feel.

He's now scared of her beauty, it's becoming too real.

She notices the change in his demeanor and reluctantly glances in the mirror.

She backs away, afraid of what he has to say.
Love was not on her agenda
so she stops her seduction in the midst of its splendor.
She looks back at the now broken man,
she knows that her seductive ways have hurt again.

Men

I need a hug from my daddy to tell me it's going to be okay, to tell me that he'll protect me, and keep the bad guys away. I need to look into his eyes to confirm what he's saying is true. I need to run and hide, from me, from you... from all of it, from everything, inside my heart screams. I cannot take it anymore. The hurt, the lies... why, why, WHY do they always have things to hide? Oh daddy, if only you could be here to protect me from scum out to break my heart, so I keep it so near, I say why, why, why did I have to be so loving, so giving, so kind, just to fall victim of love. I feel blind, I cannot see the spite they have for me, the malice in their mind, they just grind on, always on the prowl, anyway, anyhow, just to get a kiss, or a sweet voice to stroke their ego, touch their di... ugh, heck no! Not me, I will never, ever be... that girl, living in that world. Can you tell me please how to make it stop, how to keep a man from trying to mastermind a plan to break me down, lay me down, play my heartstrings like *I'm* the clown? Ugh... Daddy... you are gone, you are in the grave, you have left me torn, I am here, you are there, and these lil BOYS do not care,

that I am a lover, I am a giver, I am compassionate, but I will still hit her, who her? Yes, her. Your girlfriend her, the one you said was not anymore, the one whose jealousy my presence makes soar, I did not sign up for this, I do not date other chick's men. So hang up your phone, don't play on mine, this isn't the time for you to shine, he is not worthy of me, and for you to stay you must not be a real woman who knows her worth, cause this guy has your name in the dirt, yet still here you come looking at me, like she's a hoe, she's gotta be a freak, but know me you do not. Judge me? No, stop.
You need a mirror and some reality, and I need to be where I can see, my daddy, where he can guide me from this type of man, who looks 35 but acts all of 10... I... am so ...tired, but yet I hold on, because daddy you are gone, but you didn't leave me alone. I have my father who can't leave, who has vowed to love me endlessly. Who doesn't play games, whose name is always the same, who doesn't call my family with lies defaming my name... ahh... all this other stuff is so minute, when this kind of love is as honorable as a soldier's salute? So, hmm men step back, take notes, all your games, and lies I have the power to

revoke. I don't want your kisses or your lame excuses, I don't want your touchiness, all you'd do is abuse it... I have something greater in me, and all the ones in the past tried to keep me from being, this great woman who I am starting to be, and its way out of my hands, it's no longer up to me. So yes, I have cried, and yes, I have been down, but he has dried my tears, and is handing me my crown. I am a queen, he whispers to me, "you are beautifully and wonderfully made, my love for you goes beyond this world, so why are you worrying about silly boys and their silly girls. Daughter, do not be upset at what they have done towards you, it is not personally you, but the me living in you. Rise, be strong in the face of adversary, and anything that attacks you has to go through me. I am a very present help in a time of trouble, and I will avenge you, so stop this talk of scuffles. I command you to love all people, in every situation, no matter how much it hurts, even they are my creation. Cast all your cares to me, and I will set you free. You shall go now and have perfect peace."

Can You?

Can You hear me?
The sounds that escape my lips
Can You?
Can You remember the last time you felt my kiss?
I just...
I wish that you could
I want you to....
Touch me
Can You?
Can You feel me?
It's so warm
It's so...
Moist
My breath as I speak these lines
Can you?
...tell me you don't mind...
Laying me down
relaxing my muscles
Can you?
Share this feeling, it's so universal
I need to know
if you can -- But if you can't
Just let me go....

Crush

Hmm...I think if we talked, you'd like what I have to say,
and from one conversation, you'd ask me out one day.
But why...
When I see you, I'm not me?

I'm nervous, I'm shaking, I'm ready to flee...
I just...I remember,
do you?
Don't you?
How you looked at me at your event.
Like you'd found your one!
But just as fast as it appeared, there it went...

But I never forgot the feeling I felt
when our eyes met...
you left my mouth feeling so wet.

I was tripping with anticipation for what was to come.
Without ever touching me you had me sprung.
Maybe it's best if we don't become close.
Our bodies joined together would be like a hoax,

just too good to be true.
And right now's not a good time for me to be in love....*with you.*
Not you...
You would make me weak.
I would forget who I am, I'd no longer be complete.
But still...
Because of that intense moment I developed this crush
what scared me most, is it goes deeper than lust.

I just want you to say something, anything, tell me you don't care.
But that'd be a lie, cause your eyes say it's still there.
Ughh... this just ain't fair.

I'm going to keep on pretending like it didn't happen.
Maybe one day I'll get the right reaction.

Mind Games

Should I cry over this?
But what would that say about me?
Crying over something that was never meant to be?
Fueling the naysayers like, look, I told you, see
why I told you to guard your heart?
Why I told you to wait for God, who is more
than you in terms of smart
decisions and choices to make, you had to
take the one causing the most debate.
Just wait.
Please, just wait.
You don't need someone so much
that you can't wait.
You don't need someone so much
that your willing to give it away.
Even though it hurts now
it's going to be okay.

Attraction

He said he got what I want.
Flashing his keys around like some grade school taunt.
He grabs his package, from off his knees.
Looking me up and down, his eyes begging please.
Just to taste the way my lips smack.
Baby, can I have some of that?
I've got what you want, got what you need,
I'm like the water to your plant baby, let's make seeds.
But his heart is dirty, trifling,
filled with disease.
He doesn't have what I want, not even what I need.
But still I'm drawn into his spirit so deep.
I'm like a pigeon without central park,
lost and roaming, my soul is in the dark.
Do I think he, with his big hands and feet can quench my thirst?
Even though I know it's opposite of what I need most.
Temporary pleasure or long-lasting heartache.
It shouldn't be a hard one, but which decision to make?

Love

Is it true that we've found each other our hearts individually beat until the day they beat together? Is it real, the way you look at me, matches the way you feel? Your heart warms because I've finally succumbed to the stubborn parts of my heart that tore me from your touch that made me want to run, withdraw and never look up... I know you missed me, I missed you too. We...we could have been happy together long ago, but I was scared, so, I told you to go on and find someone more worthy, more ready, someone more emotionally steady. So, I guess this isn't really a poem about love, this has turned into a poem about me. And although love is the target, is the origin of the words myself, me, and I, is where the story unfolds. But still in all, it's true, you and I are united and like ten Bible verses, word for word I can recite your meanings, your symbolisms, your underlining undertones. Love... on this paper its four letters, but in my heart I finally met the person echoing the sound in my heart's ears, the sound I've been longing to hear... I love you…Lacy.

Lyrical Penetration

I write how I feel,
I feel how I write,
and baby you're my Tahoma delight.

See I want you in big font, size 22.
Where everyone can see us, me and you.

With the **bold** caption, highlighted, and *italicized.*
Where that oooh–aaahhh is our favorite line.
Where the indent goes deeper than Shakespeare,
Maya Angelo and even Paul Revere.

The Red Coats are coming?
While the raincoats are rising,
do you understand what my pen is prescribing?

I want you to speak the words out in the open,
an oral declaration of what I'm hoping.
What I know you want me to write.
How this ends is up to you, because you're my co-author for the night.

Let's meet at the studio

you won't need anything but your pen and your scroll,
Let's make it a masterpiece.
A beautiful display of art between you and me.

Erotica

He said, "Oh I think you like it when I touch it like that
how I bust it, bust it open, bring it, bring it back."

He thinks my sounds are from my walls being painted
with his long stroke, and the slight choke
with the wide tip brush,
"Shhh, you're too loud baby, hush!"

But what he doesn't know is I'm crying out
not from pleasure, but a guilty shout.

I know I shouldn't be tangled in these sheets,
the ins and outs,
while I'm still incomplete.

The ups and downs.
Cold backs against walls.
Waiting for showers and rivers to fall.
You think I'm in ecstasy,
when I'm actually dying from deceit.

How do you like it boo?
I don't, and I don't like you!

Not for this, not even for that
but as hard as I try to fight
I keep coming back.

Goodbye

I don't think that we should be here anymore.
I no longer feel that we should try,
In fact, today was our last goodbye.

I think I'm ready to go on now.
Tears from last march no longer resound.

No... no.
See...
I realized
there was something different in my eyes.

Another person, tugging at my heart,
yep, the one I've been ignoring from our start.
Okay..
All right...
I think I agree that you were right
Maybe there is someone better,
just... more equipped,
someone with a tighter grip
but for now... I wait.

And appreciate single days,
single holidays,
single summer nights to play.

I think... no... I know...
this is the way to go.
I feel...
Happy.

I feel
like letting go...
Part of me will miss you so...
but the greater part of me says no.
So... we'll see,
yes let's just see
what the good Lord has for me.

In the meantime, I'll let our paths cross
naturally
Just thankful this didn't end tragically.

Come Away with Me

Oh baby, there's something I'd like you to see.
A long time ago you said that you & I couldn't be,
it broke me,
broke my heart.
I wasn't prepared to let it go, to have to re-start,
and I didn't. I stayed exactly where I was, adding only more misery.
But now baby, come away with me

There's something I want you to see.

To me, in my eyes, in my prospective, it was right for us
to be together,
to work on our future plans, our joined ideas of forever.
Come away with me.
I wanted that so deeply.
You were mine; together we were destined to shine.

I put things on hold to nourish them as a unit.

But when you left, I felt as though I blew it.
I stayed in my shell, yes, my own private cocoon.
By bitter thoughts I was consumed.
When you ended my idea of us
I thought my heart and world would simultaneously bust.
Oh baby looking at you in front of me,
standing there looking picture perfect,
I guess breaking my heart really was worth it.

But baby that's not why I'm here.
I'm taking you on a journey like Paul Revere.
Into my new world, my new life.
No, I'm still nobody's girl, no ring; I'm not a wife.

But what I am is happy and complete.
It all happened when men I ceased to seek.
I replaced my compulsive need for love with a very positive seed from above.

So baby, come away with me,
to my new realities, where what used to be impossible
is now very tangible.
Where what was once so important

has taken a back seat to my newest endorsement.

Come away with me.
Let me show you how you helped set me free.

Imaginary Boyfriend

I saw us together in my thoughts before your words and mine ever combined.
You were tall, dark, and handsome, everything I want, and then some.
You said all the right things, touched me in all the right spots.
You knew exactly what to do to get me hot.

I was in trouble before it ever happened, and when it did, I wasn't able to fathom falling for someone in just my thoughts.
Falling for someone before we were ever to talk.

Oh, me oh my, how can I be falling for this imaginary guy?
This really isn't fair, because I already have someone standing there,
when he says the wrong thing, or forgets an important day,
I replace him with you in every possible way.
When I close my eyes, it is you I contrive.
To see, to be with, to hold to touch, in short, it's you who make me feel alive.
In my current relationship, I try to make him into the things I see in you

But you aren't really there, so this fictitious figure is really who?

What does it mean?
And can my relationship survive such a thing?
I sigh, sometimes I'd rather just die.
Well, actually no that's not exactly true.
But I do wish that my man could be like you.
The sad truth is that I'm in a relationship doomed to end before it began.
How unfair of me to ask my partner to live up to standards of an imaginary man.
This union can no longer be.
I need to end this relationship with you both and work on the one within me.

Pursue

I want this.
I want you.
I want you to want me, too.

I see you in the shadows of my emptiness.
I wonder if you desire to fill the pages that should tell of completeness.
But, caution, there is something missing.
Something not quite clicking.
She's got to get some things accomplished within herself, she's kind of a mess.
Lacking love, and discernment of her own gifts.

She is one of a kind, a true dime, a great find.
But she's got to know it, no, really know it for herself.
So, while you watch her and ponder how to pursue,
she is a helper, and now she wants to help you.
Save you from heartbreak,
that while she wants to be in love, she must wait.

And though she often feels lonely

she really shouldn't date.
So what is man to do, when he finds the one he wants to pursue?
Wait, wait for her to be of good courage, and pray she'll able to receive you.

Questions

Why don't you miss me? Why don't you call?
You act as if you don't miss me at all.
Was I not the best girl to enter your life?
I guess I was mistaken; I was not your idea of a wife.
Why do I care? Why do I wonder what you're doing over there?
Is it just me, or is some part of you as sad as me?
I feel as though you're out having fun,
forgetting about me as if we never begun.
I am beyond sad,
I have exceeded anger,
I have moved into resisting turning into the lone ranger.
I do not want too just be alone,
but I can't forever stay in this zone
of missing and thinking of you.
You have forgotten me; I need to forget you too.

My phone doesn't ring,
your heart no longer sings.
My name, my name.
I guess it was all a game.

Was it a game?
These questions are rhetorical.
Our relationship is historical.
Ancient history.
But how you're doing me now remains a mystery.

Unavailable

I wonder why it's always a guy who I can't
relate to,
a guy I can't expect to
fall in love with
always comes at me as his dream chick,
saying the right things,
offering his attention, affection, even love so
it seems.
But it's always missing that special spark,
the feeling that's supposed to go off in your
heart
that lets you know you've found your guy.
I can't help but wonder why
I always attract such nice, gentle*men*
who a life with, I can't begin
because of clashing religions,
unreturned feelings...
or my best friend's ex,
can't wait for sex...
So many reasons why my knight's flight has
been delayed
and these imposters have to play
with my mind,
with my heart
with my soul.

These crazy love games have taken me whole.
So I just wait, he must be close...
Closer than he was yesterday.
Our hearts are already connected in many ways.
I am his and he is mine.
And I can wait for my connection, divine.

I'm Ready

It's been so many years that I've been waiting and anticipating the touch of the man God has promised me. To his feel, his hand gripping my hand, laying me down, undoing my clothes, making love to my mind. It goes so far beyond a bump and grind. I want to physically undress you, mentally, take off all your layers, pull you into me, deeper, much deeper, beyond the tip, beyond the dip of my back as it curves under the pressure of you pushing against my dresser. I want to undress you, seduce your thoughts into verbally penetrating my garden, taking me for a ride, then all of a sudden, I'm higher than I've ever been, lower than I thought I could ever go. I'm so in love with your touch, I want you so much, so bad, I'm so ...aroused at the sound of your voice, your words glide through my valley, taking the scenic route, it's been so long since anyone's been here, but there's no drought, it's so wet... my appetite for you, it's dangerously slippery... don't fall. Watch your step or you just might stumble into me. What is your ultimate fantasy? Because you evoke every sense of mine, from your stare to your hair, to the way your package bulges from down there. I'm ready... I'm ready for your ecstasy, baby... my baby... let's make a baby. A little you, a little you, a beautiful mixture between us two. She'll have my hair, he'll have your eyes, they both will come at the same time, surprise!! We've waited this long, we may as well have a double feature, but double the work means double the pleasure, so... it's time to go because I'm ready, there's no stopping me. And the good news is that I waited for you. I held off the leeches, yes babe, I practice what I preach... no ring, no ding, but once the dress comes off, there goes the rest. Our clothes nothing but a messy pile on the floor, I'm considered a goody-goody church girl, but tonight we're doing it like I'm a common day whore... Oooh, no she didn't... you're right, I didn't because you're not here, but once we exchange our vows, no holding back my dear. I'm ready...

It's Done

Today it was done.

A new development in me has begun.
My dependency,
recovery,
urgency?
To prove you were wrong,
those feelings are gone.
I **know** I'm a good girl,
a *great catch*.
But I felt you didn't realize it,
Can you imagine that?
Anyway, it has happened again, how can this be?
No matter how hard I try, they just don't see the treasure they *had* in me!
And *rejection*....
Is a feeling that confuses my pride.
How can you not want *me?* Your heart **must** be blind.
Thoughts of reversing the feelings began to fill my veins,
where I try to compensate the rejection over and over again
with meaningless affairs that pull at my validation,

makes me I feel alive and gives some sort of vindication
giving pieces of my body to men who didn't deserve it!
All so I can feel that someone see's I'm worth it.
Oh the agony deep within.
There was no sex, but yet I still sinned against my own soul...
Believing the lies the enemy told.
Watching the decay allowing his plan to unfold.
I let him in; I let the foothold take root.
I allowed someone's actions to clog up and pollute
my view...
For losing yourself isn't so hard to do
when you feel that everyone has what they want; everyone but you!
That you're a good person and tired of being passed by
when somehow you become blinded by false light.
But I have decided to get my mind off those things.
Off the feelings of anger that rejection brings.
The validation, vindication, payback… or… just understanding.

Can't, doesn't and won't ever come from false connections that are too demanding. Of my time, energy and emotions And give my heart back to God with pure love, commitment and devotion.

POEMS ABOUT MY RELATIONSHIP WITH GOD

Therapy

Can you see the change in me?
In comes from self-therapy.
I don't have a counselor
but I know God is a prayer answerer.
Helping rid me of my inadequacies
and reveal all the hidden struggles I could not see.
How did this change come about?
I simply got tired of all the pain, emptiness and drought.
Bitterness of broken relationships
and the rejection of being forsaken and easily dismissed.
I was fed up with my lack of finances,
despondent of being too afraid to take chances,
ashamed of my instability,
sad from always trying to be
something, anything that will bring about change.
Change that will lift the heavy strain.
Disgraced from always trying to fit in.
Exasperated from having to start over and try again.
With my last break up, I knew I needed to get help.

I knew there were ways to overcome how I felt
Feelings of questioning who, when, what and why
and never having an answer to who am I?
The torment of having dreams without the courage to pursue
Annoyed at hearin', *I'm a do me, so why don't you do you.*
Sadly, I didn't have a me to represent
because I was too full of resentment.

From this therapy I know I will gain a new perspective,
a new lease on life, how to love and respect it.
To no longer hoard life's disappointments
to begin to enjoy and embrace life's appointments.
With this therapy there is a new person inside,
I hope you'll stay along for the finished surprise.

It

It is like an empty midnight sky
with no stars shinning down to wave
goodbye.

It is a tempting mystery
yet no one approaches, due to its history.
Its blinding rage is like a bull running full
pace
charging anyone or anything who tries to take
its place.

It's not so simple to unplug its power.
The ones who have tried, have been
devoured.

It is like rain drops at an evening wedding,
the show must go on but there's no forgetting.

It is what truly happens when we give up on
our dreams.
It is the sounds we hear when our nightmares
scream.

It has been everywhere and seen everything.
It is the only thing standing in between---
joy and sorrow.

It even has the power to steal the hope for tomorrow.

Just what is it you ask?
It's a spirit of lack
and of brokenness,
accompanied and carried by its brother hopeless.

It can happen anytime with a very grim chance to renew
So the best offense is not to let *it* happen to you.

The Light

You deserve the best I have to give,
all my affection, in return for your protection.
How many nights I cried in my bed
for someone to deliver me from my desire to
no longer live, my desire to be dead?
I have been through so many people, people
who were supposed to be there,
through thick and thin,
but somehow relationships with those would
always end.
I have done some horrible things,
yet you see past that, and this love is serene.
Great are your mercies towards me.
Great is Your grace.
How You allow me to keep seeking your
face.
For the answers of how to survive.
Though I sometimes fall, I will continue to
strive
to give You, my Lord, my savior, my friend,
the best of me, surpass my ability, to
transcend
the fears I've always held within,
because you died, now You live through me.
A friendship with benefits beyond what the
naked eye can see.

Lord, I love you.
Lord, I need You.
Lord, please search me.
Help me to please You.
Without you, there is no me.
Without Your partnership, I cannot be righteous, humble, renewed spiritually.
Lord, I thank You for your covenant relationship with a wretch like me.

True Love

It's taken me all this time to realize it's You
who I've been craving, needing, wanting,
hoping for, desiring,
thinking I would go on without finding, true
intimacy, my hopes were expiring.
I never imagined I, Z. Lacy Cole, would ever
feel this way. Could have something to look
forward to, inspiration for a new day.
We met before, but I played a game.
I pretty much knew you, at least who you
were and your name,
but I ran from getting close to You, thinking
that someone else would do.
And those love-ships always started right,
but when they'd end, it was you I lie in bed
thinking of at night.
Remembering how You wanted to be there,
to show me, that with You I could always
share
my deepest fears and concerns,
how I want to love but I'm afraid of being
burned.
I remember how You told me that in You I
could trust,
that Your strong enough to handle me,
even my issues with lust.

But still I ran from you,
I couldn't get too close
because to me you represented everything
that I want most.

To love, to be loved, to be free.
Free of everything, free from me.

So how could I let you in?
Uncover myself yet again?
I didn't want you to see what I see in myself.
Beautiful outside while the inside's a mess.

No—I couldn't handle it.
So the less than perfect unions are where I
chose to commit.
It took losing them for me to see
that as each relationship fell apart, with them
went intricate pieces of my heart and me.
Things I can never get back, and with their
loss, it's hard for me not to react.
But it was in those moments where I
remembered you,
and during this time people said that you
were thinking of me, too.
So, with puffy, drained eyes, and a restless
body

I gathered enough strength to call, hoping a chance to talk, You wouldn't deny me.
With an open heart, You listened as I shared my countless blunders.
You were so kind, so loving, so tender.
You held me close and let me know that before You can forgive me, I have to forgive myself.
That I can stop crying because I'm no longer alone in the midst of distress.
When I told You I felt like a failure of love
You reminded me that together we'll fit as snug as a glove.
When I showed signs of disbelief
You promised that you'd always protect me from my joy's thief.
Even when I got so upset that I couldn't speak
You told me how pleased you were at my surrender of being meek.
Our convo ended with the birth of something wonderful,
a connection so deep that can only be described as spiritual.
As I allow my heart to free fall into your capable hands,
chest beaming proudly of my wonderful man,
I smile because I'm finally complete.

To love, I have finally been released.
Jesus, you heard my cry
and now I know I can make it with you by my side.
Thank you for never leaving nor forsaking me.
Thank you for saving a wreck like me.

Thank you for being not only my friend,
But the true lover of my soul, my spiritual husband.

Cheating

He touches the nape of my neck with the small of his fingertip.
My body begins to quiver, I tingle, it tingles,
together we begin a journey of tainted pleasure.

As he looks into my eyes, I see nothing there.
I am emotional, I want this, I want to feel this,
I want to feel his touch; I want to be taken away.

All I feel is pleasure,
but all I feel is pain.
I can't even bear the thought of me,
I am cheating on you,
my love, how could I forsake you in this way?

With this man who doesn't deserve my touch,
yet alone my love. My dedication.

I yearn for you when I am with him.
I think of you when he touches me.
You deserve better.

You deserve better than to love a cheater like me,
but yet you do.

With great compassion and deep concern,
you stay by my side.
You hold me when I come home from a night being with him,
And tell me everything is going to be okay.

I don't know if I could ever love anyone the way you love me.
I don't know if I could forgive anyone as easily as you forgive me,
every single day.
But I strive to.

I strive to get back with you,
and love you the way you love me.

I don't want to cheat on you,
but I feel as though I am trapped

Your love is so overwhelming,
I'm not sure if I can handle someone loving me in that way,
so I cheat, but it's not just on you, for I'm also cheating myself.

Of something so beautiful, something I've always wanted.
True intimacy.
True Love.

How backwards and bizarre the very thing that I desire,
I run from.

Because you love me, it makes me want to love myself more.
So I ask, with all that I have, for to you to take me back,
and help me to lean on you for all that I need,
To trust you, because you truly do know what's best.

My love, from this day forward
I'm Done Cheating,
I love you.

Peace of Mind

Peacefully, I'm whole again.
He washed me, he loved, he restored me
and my faith in mankind.
I am refurnished, rejuvenated.
I am free to love, free to give, free to see the
blessings all around me.
What is my strongest desire?
It used to be marriage,
yes the union of two lives,
but I think I wanted that most because it
would validate me.
It would get others off my back and from
thinking, I am incomplete.
It would keep others from thinking there is
something wrong with me
There's nothing wrong with me besides me,
besides me not living my life.
But that's all over now, for now I am free.
And to get married is a thing I no long desire.
But to enjoy being single, to live in the
moment and enjoy each day…as it is.
Without trying to make it what I desire it to
be,
Yes, this is my ultimate dream and now
I have what it takes to make this dream
complete.

I am bold,
I am secure,
I am a writer
a risk–taker,
task–oriented,
free-spirited
fun.
An over comer
I am peacefully whole again.

The Door

My daughter, please open the door.
There is great urgency for me to free you,
to release your mind,
to help you let go.

My daughter, please open the door.
As I stand here knocking
my spirit is calling out to you,
do you not hear my voice?
Do you not understand that your pain is My pain?

My daughter, please open the door.
I'm the only one who can save you,
I'm the only one who can mend your broken heart.
I'm the only one with love powerful enough
to fill every void,
every open wound, only I can heal,
every tear, only I can wipe away.

My daughter, please open the door.
Why do you run from me?
Do you understand that I am unlike all the others?

That I am the only one who can earnestly say
I'll never leave you,
I'll never forsake you.
I'll never lie.
Never break your heart.

My daughter, please open the door.
Let me in.
Let me breathe life into your darkness.
Let me give you peace of mind.
Security.
Love.
My daughter, please open the door.
I can't come in until you invite Me.
I can't take my rightful seat in your heart
until you give permission.
I will not invade your space.
I will not give you more than you can bear.
I will not ask you to go any place that I
haven't gone Myself.

My daughter, please open the door.
My daughter, please open your heart.
My daughter, please don't give up.
My daughter, dear child.
Will you open the door for Me today?

Holy Ghost

Father.
Son,
Spirit.
the Holy Ghost.
An invisible,
voiceless,
incredible
wonder.
Sent from God himself to abide in the world.
Wow.
Remarkable.
How God loves us so.
Not only did he give us His son,
but a spirit we can always call on.
Friend.
Counselor.
Doctor.
Only God can do something this incredible.
Only God can love with such intensity,
a constant reminder of His greatness.
I am nothing without my father.
Who has given me His,
son
and His
spirit.

Period

Father. Son. Spirit.

The father gave his son,
who shed his blood and left His spirit:
an invisible,
voiceless,
incredible
wonder...
A
teacher,
transformer,
habit changer.
Friend.
Counselor.
Doctor.
Holy, Holy, Holy.
Holy Father
Holy Son.
Holy Ghost.

This World, That World

This morning I woke up feeling free.
Like there was nothing standing in front of me.
Nor behind, nor on the side, just me free to enjoy the ride.
The ride of life, and true liberty,
Where I am not concerned of what you think of me.
For I was delivered from the pressures of this world
where there is less pressure on boys than there are on girls
to be perfect, to not be promiscuous.
To openly sit down and have a discussion about this,
to be proud of the fact that I do not drink, nor do I smoke
anything
but let me not boast...
For me to have true stability
comes from a source much higher than me.
Yes, I am talking about divine intervention from that world.
The world, which sits higher than the trees above,
to keep me steadfast in heavenly bliss.

And the Holy Spirit is with me so I do not miss
any opportunity to share the joys of the Lord,
in which I do not have to fight, I have given him my sword.
Where I do not have to fret, He's taken my mind off all of that.
All of what you ask?
The pain of confusion I no longer have to mask.
The questions of who, what, when, and why, for He has given me all the answers to survive this life.
Where this world cannot function without a visit from the throne
And while, that world abides in me, it is here in this world that my body roams.

It's Time

It's Time, It's Time,
to do something new.
For making friends with yourself can be fun too.

It's Time, It's Time,
to let your hair down.
To be the queen you are and embrace your inner crown.

It's Time, It's Time,
to be who you were born to be.
Time to stop wasting time being incomplete.

It's Time, It's Time,
to chuck the deuces.
Let go of all the bad examples and negatives influences.

It's Time, It's Time,
to know who it is you should invest in and seek.
To be the person you want to meet.

It's Time, It's Time,
to let go of fear and let your inner light shine.
It's Time.

Dear God

I don't know if this will translate but that's the beauty of being your friend, because you can always relate. I can't stomach how bad this feels at times, but it is the result of my self-loathing crimes. So I'll try not to complain, I'll try to keep my thoughts in line and avoid going insane. I now know why I avoided these changes for so long, as each friendship has come and gone, I realize some of the reasons why I cry, why I lay alone at night.

It's hard to face the truth of your mistakes, but I know that I can overcome by your grace. I know that it'll be worth it all in the end, I just wish I didn't have to be isolated to begin. I know, I know, this is all a part of your plan, and I am learning to really trust you as my ultimate man. The main source of my security, to rely on you for all my needs. It's just, wow, I thought I was lonely before, before I pushed all the people in my life through a closed, sealed door. I thought they were friends; men mature enough not to follow the cheating trend. But what I did, I had to do, I just wish I would have allowed it to bring me closer to You. But it just made me search for their replacements. People, who would embrace me and see my worth, validate me and give me hope.

Each time I found someone new; in my mind I guess I did look to them instead of You. The new blessing that would agree with me that I am great, look forward to my phone calls, and anticipate my company without any haste. But it seems it's always **ME,** striking up the phone calls and doing whatever to please. I want to be the one who is pursued, tired of the one always feeling subdued. All these instances have left me feeling weak, which made me afraid to follow your command of being meek.

Chasing friendships has only made me more insecure, which was the prime reason my latest relationship couldn't endure, my irrational thoughts, my unwarranted fears, my ex-boyfriend just couldn't understand my tears. I focused on improving him and us, I never once tried to work on my lack of trust, in people as a whole, I just went on focusing on marriage as a goal.

I know this work you're doing in me is for a greater purpose. Therefore, I'm trying to just relax and let you work it. Fill all this time I have doing the things I should have done before, while anticipating all the things you have in store, for me, and my whole family. I know this change your doing is what I should be focused on pursuing, so I am, but it's just so hard. I'm taking college algebra and it's got me feeling like a retard—sorry father, I know all people are your creation, and to speak against them like that would bring the end to my duration, so forgive me, let me retract that statement, what I should have said is that this math class has been one of the hardest things to present, to my family as one of my goals, in which I feel my lack of effort has taken a toll on my ability to dream big, I have felt as though to win, it would have to be rigged.

But I know that on this journey to become the woman you created me to be, to go back to the drawing board, allowing myself to see, that I have to endure these things as a soldier, because I know all things are possible through you, great Jehovah. When it gets hard, I won't look to men, or to those with whom I wish to fit in. No longer will I take the easy way out, hoping for someone to come along and see my pout. Feel sorry, or empathy, and give me the things I feel I need. No, I will continue to do what's hard, knowing that the process is one of the best rewards. I have avoided this for as long as I can remember, and who knows where my life will be by December. All I know is that I want a different outcome, one with health and wealth, friends, love and then some. I know that everything I desire is already inside, I just have to trust that you'll make everything all right.

I love You.

Free to Write Part Three

I've felt happier lately than the times mentioned before,
and what do you know, depression knocks at my door.
I spoke to my ex the other night, his voice was refreshing to my hunger, what a delight.
But afterwards, the pain began again.
Oh how I really do miss him…
He made a good point, that I seemed happy now that we're over,
but talking to him just reminded me of how much I miss lounging on his shoulder.
Or just having someone there,
someone for this overwhelming loneliness to share.
Someone to hold, and someone to kiss.
Someone to long for, someone to miss.
It was nice to know that he's been craving me too
or perhaps I just allowed myself to think that perceptions can be cruel.
Dear Lord, my soul thirst for this process to end,
missing the affection and the touch of a man.
I was beginning to feel content,
then he shows up and it's back to resentment

for what I'm going through,
but I know these feelings are unfair to you.
Do many women suffer with this?
I know I cannot get off course or I will miss
my real chance of love and fulfillment.
I understand that this process is going to
make me resilient,
and not be so desperate for things I don't
have
and long for friendships and relationships that
didn't last.

I am relying on your love and support,
leaning on you I will resort,
turning away from immediate gratification,
which only added to my grief's
multiplication.
I love that you have given me an outlet in
writing,
it's so much easier than exercising or hiking.
But I know I need to do that too,
it's so many changes I'm making to bring me
through. So I will be strong, I will continue to
walk in peace
knowing that in your love is true liberty.
I will not act on feeling love sick,
I will get back on task and will not resist

you… I need you,
and trust that you will bring me through.
I love You.

Butterfly

Like colorful lilies flying high
through the valley the Lord ordained the sky.
Innocent as a baby bird before its wings.
As beautiful as the voice of an angel's beam
of light, decorating the world like the smile of
a girl
who once lost her way,
trapped in the darkness of spiritual decay.
The butterfly has no recognition of hurt,
abuse, abandonment
or the bitter sting or resentment.
How sufficient, magnificent, brilliant,
resilient;
the way the butterfly shaves its shell,
emerging from its cocoon with a story to tell.
Butterfly.

Really?

I'm having difficulty writing about this.
I guess it's because I've never quite
experienced
true contentment,
true enjoyment,
I am becoming free.
And can honestly say that I am happy.

It didn't come from having a man
or seeing the benefits of working my plan.
No, I just chose to believe that I actually can
stop crying, doubting, wondering, and
worrying.

And now I am seeing a different side of
living,
where I'm comfortable in my skin, free
spirited and forgiving.

Can it be? Can this really be?
That satisfied person in the mirror is me?
I'm happy?
I'm free?
This is *my* heart full of glee?

The last time I began to feel good
my ex came back and there I stood,
longing for him, completely drained,
not being able to sleep, not even through the rain.

So – is this real?
Is this the new way my mind will feel?
I hope so.
I…believe so.
I pray... so...
NO... I KNOW so…

Only time will tell,
but for now I am doing QUITE well.

Deadly Sin

I stand unclothed at a busy intersection. Vehicles whiz by me in great anticipation. They look back in wonder at my naked blunder, I begin to walk further into traffic knowing the possibility of this ending tragic. But fear eludes me, my eyes can only see, one thing, just one thing. The other side it's blindingly bright and there is something within, pulling so tight. Walk further, walk further it says--walk further, walk further you can't renege.

With eyes wide shut, I make one final step; the power of the impact has left me limp. There is nothing, no sounds. No one is around. I am not awake, yet I am not sleep. I am being held in a room that's dark, and deep.

Something begins to gnaw at my fingertips, it has now come and stood over me, it's presence a deadly grip. I can't open my eyes, I can't even cry. I try to talk, but my throat is too dry.
"She's Mine!" I heard a powerful voice declare.

"No, no, no…she didn't trust you while she was there.
So as she took that final step,
my dark angels began to prep."
"She belongs to me!" the first voice began.
"Well that was before her deadly sin!"

Smoke begins to fill my lungs.
"My dear child, what have you done?"

My insides begin to melt as the heat from the fire burns with no regret.
Help me, help me, please--I try to speak, but the smoke continues to squeeze
my lungs--my eternity of torture has begun.

The powerful voice is becoming harder to hear, I realize that he's moving away from here,
but quietly, I stilled my body.
"All you had to do was follow me."
His words resound through my being,
"My Holy Spirit was your only source of fleeing.

I told you I would give you peace
all you had to do was keep your mind on me."

"Leave here now; it's too late to save her!
She is now my eternal prisoner."

Noooo, I tried to scream, I tried to reach out to my heavenly king, but he had already died once for me. And I ignored his attempts to further set me free.
So the day I took my own life, I really paid the ultimate price.

I thought it would make all my pain go away, but now I am forced to burn here day after day. If I could go back, I would face my demons, I would seek Jesus and take in his reasons, to do it his way, to pray and pray and pray.
So that instead of laying here unable to speak, unable to see I'd be alive and living, happy and carefree.

"My child, I will still love you and cherish your memory,
for now maybe you'll understand how much you meant to me.
Our father has given you free choice,
but at your decision neither of us rejoice.

I must leave now, but I pray that those who hear your story will choose a different way."

Reunited...

Oh...I didn't think I'd find my way back to you...
I've been gone doing my own thing,
but lately...
lately, I just crave you...

I think about you at the still of the night,
when my heart beats slow and nothing feels right.
I remember feeling like... man... he deserves better.
Like... he's the best man I've ever known
and I'm a wreck. I'm best on my own.

But here I am...
Wondering how to get back...
Just get back to you...
See you again...
You know... have our long talks,
and our late-night walks.
Before I ran away from your love...

It's kinda silly, but I think you have forgiven me.
I think you want me back, too...
Actually I dun think you ever left me.

And I know you never stopped caring...
Dare I say... you never even stopped loving me...
I thought maybe I could find your kind of love somewhere else...
But... as you can see... I was wrong.

So what I'm saying is...
I wanna get back together...
We can take it slow,
cause I just need to know.

Do you want me to,
reenact loving you?
Jesus, my Lord... I know you do...
So here I am...
running back to you.

Weak

I am weak.
I need to hear from you.
Just a whisper will do.
In my body, there is nothing but decay,
unless you tell me you're here to stay.
Please don't allow my selfish ways to end our relationship,
I just need help getting equipped.
I know that I can change,
but it's so touching how you'll love me even if I stay the same.
But you see? That's the thing,
your love makes me want to be the queen.
You said I was born to be,
it makes me want to be a better me...
I just want to be where you are.
I'm so weak.
So, so weak
for a glimpse of you, I'll even settle for a peek.
Please.
I need you more and more.
I'm so in love, you're my mi amore.
Just your presence makes me feel that I'm okay.

And that my pains and troubles will get better
one day.
You are my savior,
Jesus, how can I ever repay you?
All I can do is offer you my life
in exchange for your ultimate sacrifice.
Teach me, how to be more like you
to love those around me in all I do.
To forgive, and also forget.
Stop being a contentious woman and be legit.
These things are the way to your heart.
But you don't have to say anything…
I was weak for you from the start.

Pain

It's holding me,
so tight,
so close
I can't undo it, there's no reverse.
It just grabs at my body like a shark gasping
for blood,
leaving me starving like a plant waiting to
bud.
It's not easy,
being humble, being sweet,
being open, vulnerable and insecure,
trying not to let it control me anymore.
I just cry and pray,
and pray and cry,
lay flat on the bed and close my eyes,
but the pain,
the misery,
surrounds me...
my insides scream aloud.
Just let me be!
A small voice whispers,
The only way out is through **Me!**
I am knocking, let me in so I can set you free!
JESUS, Jesus, Jesus.
You *ARE*
my deliverer!

Hope

Don't be discouraged,
it's all gonna be okay.

Dry your eyes little baby,
the pain's gonna walk away.

Seems unfair, like everyone else gets to live their dreams,
while the same people sit around laughing over your screams.

You think there's no point in trying,
your soul, your spirit, your mind is dying.
But...
bitter feelings sometimes provoke
hope.

Simple...

It's simple,
you are my light and true example
of love♥.

Lyrics...

Little baby don't be scared,
dry your eyes,
you know the Lord, he really cares,
everything will be alright.
It's just a challenge,
just a little test,
sometimes you go through the bad times
to appreciate the best.
So...
look to the hills,
from when cometh your help...
Shut out negativity,
look forward to something else.

Experience Him for Yourself

You can't see the invisible.
Can't hear the unspoken sounds of a voiceless man.
All you can do is believe and trust, that God knows all, and rely on His plan.
You see friends, He has given us many gifts.
One His son, one His spirit.
One once lived as man, one whom will never touch land.
But He abides in all of us. Yes, even you.
People will say it's a myth, that it's not true.
But He is everything you need him to be, teacher, helper, counselor, friend.
I have experienced the phenomenon over and over again.
Don't take my word for it, experience Him for yourself.
Cry out, "Holy Ghost, help!" and watch Him do the rest.
You need to be filled to get through the day.
When someone does you wrong,
He'll help you watch what you say.
He'll help you stay focused.
Teach you what love is.
When you feel like you can't,
He'll remind you that you can.

When you want to give up.
He'll simply hold your hand.
When you don't know what to say,
Just open your mouth, He'll lead the way.

Don't take my word for it, experience Him for yourself
Cry out, "Holy Ghost, help!" and watch Him do the rest.

Sculpture Park

Its beauty astounds the very grounds that flat toes under the bellows grace, with the ever-fading light of the day. I am in awe of its glory, its height, and its depth, the angle of its story. How talented, creative, boisterous, *disturbed*? The author screaming out of a vision unheard.

I can't even pretend to be on that level, the elevation, the clarification, the personification of such *creation*. Giant men with numbered chest, and red bellowing statutes that get no rest, with foot prints, hand prints, words that don't belong, and unsung lyrics to unfinished songs.

Hundreds, thousands, millions of blades, art stretching on for days, and days, and days. I was left so amazed. Ten singles supposed to mingle within the beauty, so soothing, too relaxing to be wooed by unenthused macking. Too serene to fall for the boy with the hidden heart so mean. To pretty to scur me with tainted words unworthy.

Today *love* was shown beyond blue skies

unknown to the eyes, beyond their empty soul cries, it was found beyond trees with the multicolored leaves, and beyond the red piping for everyone's liking, love was found beyond the ground where the rocks drew hearts in the grass, beyond proposals for marriage that may or may not last. Today in all its essence of the art, the beauty of *love* was found all around, from the end to the start.

Protect Your Mind

Protect my mind.
Guard my heart.

Lord, you give me authority, but making wise decisions is a good start.
With the help of the spirit, my guiding force, you help me know who to trust and when enough is enough.

I have to be mindful of who and what I entertain
unless I want old habits and attitudes to resurface again.

I have been made new, a fresh start, a new creation.
And there's no better tool of influence than information.
Rather it comes from music, peers, movies, or even my own thoughts.
I reserve the right to cast down anything that doesn't align with the cross.

My soul delights in your majesty,
but if my mind isn't right then how can I be the witnessing tool for others to see.

Your glory, your divine mercy, and favor for the lost to come to You and know You as *their* savior.

Reminder

Pull me up then pull me back, never thought
I'd fall like that.
But now I can't imagine being anywhere else,
loving anyone more than I love myself.

It's always been about me.
Now I know what selfless means.
I couldn't imagine not caring for you…

Now I see that loving you doesn't have to
mean avoiding me
and who and what I was created to be.
It's no secret that when I am with someone, I
give *them* my all,
and everything I dreamed up for myself
begins to fall.

I learned something this go around though,
that my self-esteem determines my worth
not you, and not the one before.
Not the moments from my childhood of me in
pain on the floor,
laying there, contemplating the end.
But suicide is a sickening word, that
shouldn't have an origin.

But it does…
And many suffer from its drug.
The allure that it will make everything all right.
How sad that not even your own life deserves a fight.

So as I work on me, I am beginning to see just how to love you, while *also* loving me.
It can be done
I'm worth it, I deserve it, I was made to be loved.
That's my new song.
So sometimes, you try to creep back in, get me down on myself, feeling worthless as sin.
But as you try to pull me down, his hand pulls me up and reminds me of his crown.
The thorns he proudly wore on the cross for me
And reminds me that I still have much more life to see.

My Help

My eyes are open, but I cannot see,
there is nothing when I look into me.
I've tried to find myself in so many things,
so many places... friends, family, men
but there I stood still empty.

Even in the day, it was dark
bitterness and pain overshadowed my heart.
I thought people had forsaken me.
Rejected me...
Destroyed me...
Who I was and who I wanted to be.

Soon I found that there is no me in the world,
that the true me was formed before I was
even a girl.
In their eyes, I was lost
like a puppy looking for someone to accept
my spots.
But in Christ I found the key to unlock the
mystery
that love was walking around right alongside
of me.
Wiping the tears as I cried myself to sleep,
holding me tight when I refused to eat.

Being my strength when I felt I couldn't go on.
Going before me in every sit-u-ation.

God's love has restored the peace in my mind.
Helped me love from within, to myself be kind.
In Christ Jesus, I have found where joy begins
and through the same love where isolation ends.

Uncomfortable

Lord God,
I don't know what's ahead of me, but I know where You have me now, it feels so foreign. I don't know where I am, who I am, what I'm doing, or why... this place you have me in at times makes me want to cry. Cry out to You, asking for your hand, yes Daddy, hold my hand. You have me doing all these new things, without any training or sometimes warning... Lord, why? Yes... in my heart, I want to ask why, but I've lived long enough to know that it isn't wise. You are God almighty... You know the plans You have for me. Rather I understand it or not, I know You will not let me rot, in this place that feels bizarre to me. There are no crutches, nowhere for me to hide. I truly am uncomfortable to my core; I'm holding my breath to the point my jaws feel sore. I know you are getting me ready, I know this process isn't just for me, so I'm trying to be strong, trying to hang in there, but I feel like I'm being prematurely called into warfare.

I don't like being embarrassed or made to look like a fool. But I feel the way I felt when

I was back in school. I want preparation for the preparation. Supply the materials to study for the test. Lord please don't let me be stranded in this alone. If you called me to do these things, Lord give me the guidance. Give me the knowledge. I lean on you, Lord. I am completely lost, completely helpless... LORD GOD... I can't do this if you don't do it through me. I can't speak the words if you don't speak through me. Father God, it's just so uncomfortable. My soul cries out so, not to remove me, but prepare me. Help me see what it is you want to show me, help me to learn what it is you're trying to teach me. Help me get through this season QUICKLY, Lord keep me from expanding my season of learning, keep my mouth from overturning my blessings... in this out of comfort zone level, that I will come out and people will marvel...

Knowing that I went in with some timidity and fear and walk out leaving behind all covetousness. All is well, all is well. I say it in my soul, "Yes, Lord all is well." My discomfort is just a new opportunity to be blessed. So I take it all in stride, counting it all Joy. I may be uncomfortable, yet I remain

humble, knowing that You will never leave,
nor forsake me, because You love me so, You
promised you'd never leave, so
uncomfortable I'll be.

Fire Around Me

What is this?
Am I awake or asleep?
All I know is there is fire around me.
The trees bow and bend and bend and bow,
the trumpets sound off as the river flows.
Am I awake or am I sleep?
All I know is there is fire around me.
I speak what I see, and what I see is a figure,
a strange character hovering over a man who
needs to be delivered.
The eyes are dark; the soul is too,
who is this person, it's not me, is it you?
The figure moves its disfigured body in
circles around the temple.
I grab its horn, this thing is scorned
because I don't know if I'm woke or sleep;
all I see is fire around me.
I take the fire burning in my midst,
throw it on the figure and send it back to the
abyss.
I'm not afraid to war in the spirit, rather I'm
awake or rather I'm sleep
I know the fire burning is there to protect me.

The Sound

The Trumpet Sounds and now I can hear clearly
the person who has always been inside of me, the little lost girl looking for love has been plucked up out of depression by the Lord above.
This sound that came from Heaven nearly knocked me down.
"My child, My child, follow me."
In my own knowledge I was blind to self and the lies of the enemy looking back in my reflection. I thought I had it all together, I knew God, Jesus, the Holy spirit, we all hung out together.
But, lo...
I was free in disguise. Left to my own demise
What I thought I knew couldn't compare to what this sound imparted to me.
The things I thought I saw before, did not prepare me for what God really had in store for this little self-imposed lonely girl trapped in the fantasy of romance chasing the thought of being swept off my feet.
My God in Heaven had a real gut check for me.

"My child, My child, follow Me."
"Yes, my Lord, I hear you now,
My ears have been cleaned out, now I'm able to hear Your sound
Now I understand the gifts You've put on the inside of me
Now I can see the things You've been trying to show me."
"He that hath ears to hear, let him hear"
But how can you hear him when you're so full of fear my dear?
I realized the things I desired and wanted were within my reach,
but I had to first let go of self, be humble, listen and let him teach.
Each heartache, each breakup, each time feeling discouraged...
every time I looked in the mirror and felt embarrassed,
every tear dripped in despair,
every diary page holding the years of pain I felt I couldn't bear,
everything that was bad, God turned it for my good.
I was not rejected, maybe a little misunderstood,
but God protected and kept me through it all.

And now I'm able to share my story, throw my shoulders back and stand tall.

I Love You, Jesus

There's a popular song that I love to sing, the verses are so simple but it speaks to me.
It's all about loving Jesus more than anything.
Some of my loved ones don't understand this song in my heart. But I can't explain it to them because I've known from the start, since I was a very young child I've known and loved Jesus, and to try to explain it, I found it to be very strategic. But it wasn't until the death of my father where I went through a hard time and it seemed there was nothing I could do to ease my mind... I was sad, I was hurting, I was empty inside and I looked to the world to quench my cries,
I wanted to feel loved again, I wanted to feel embraced by a man,
I missed being the apple of someone's eye and I didn't really want to get that type of feeling from a big God in a big sky…
I tried from eating my feelings, to pushing my friends away. So I looked to men as my final escape.
I tried to date,
and date…
and date,

but ended up feeling worse than I did before, I even dubbed myself as a 'date whore'. I didn't give them my body, I rarely even gave out kisses, yet still I was reserved for dates, instead of being someone's misses...
It wasn't until I called on the name of Jesus that I was set free,
so I do not mean to offend anyone with my beliefs, but I'm grateful that your disbelief also doesn't offend me. There used to be a time when I'd argue about his goodness to those who said he wasn't he, but I realized that arguing was not to prove to him but to prove me. So now I just pray for their deliverance so they can receive the free gift of salvation and not miss their entrance into Heaven's gates. I know my beliefs negates a lot of hate from those who don't know me personally

but those who do just go on their way respecting my ideas and listening to what I have to say. We agree to disagree and that's okay with me. I love my friends and family, but I desire for them to also give up their vices and be set free.
If you could see what I see, I think you'd see things differently. I'm usable for the kingdom

now. But I take no credit, standing ovation, he gets to bow. So don't pray to be like me, pray to be like He who lives through me. Thank you for taking a glimpse inside my shell, God bless you all.

The Night is as Bright as the Day

Confident. Bold. Assertive.
Joyful noises are the only sounds.
Surrounding me.
There is Joy.
There is hope.
I am a beautiful virtuous creation.
Even with eyes wide shut,
the night is as bright as the day.
This is my life.
Brave. Equipped. Content.
He walks with me. He listens to me.
Breathing freshness into my soul.
I cry; he wipes my tears.
I shout. He rejoices with me.
He will never forsake me.
Never leave me.
Never leave me.
Even with eyes wide shut,
the night is as bright as the day.
This is my life.
Intuitive. Strong. Complete.
He accepts me.
He embraces me.
He sees me.
He knows my name.
He is there.

He loves me.
He rejoiced at my surrender.
He responded to His name.
Sweet, Sweet, Jesus.
Thank you for saving me.

About the Author

Dr. Z. Lacy Cole is an entrepreneur who loves God & thrives on helping others grow, learn, and prosper! She ventured into writing to express her inner world and connect to others who have or will travel similar journeys.

105 Publishing LLC
www.105publishing.com
Austin, Texas

www.ingramcontent.com/pod-product-compliance
Lightning Source LLC
LaVergne TN
LVHW051607070426
835507LV00021B/2818